# San Francisco Daddy

One Gay Man's Chronicle of His Adventures in Life and Love

Charles St. Anthony

San Francisco

Copyright 2014

Published by Impossibly Glamorous Studios

ISBN 978-0-9983185-1-6

First Edition

Edited by Marcella Hammer

Cover illustration by Terry Blas

Disclaimer:

Names, details and locations have been changed to protect the anonymity of people in these pages. This memoir involves actual people I have met and experiences I have lived through. As a work of creative nonfiction, in some cases, accounts have been paraphrased or embellished for purposes of parody or comic effect. Luckily, the reality of life in San Francisco is far funnier than anything I could possibly make up.

Some characters are composites which means I took references to several people and mashed them up into one person for ease of narrative.

# The Contents

The Mongolian She-Beast ................................................................ 1

From Twink to Daddy ..................................................................... 7

The Gummy Bear Ghetto ............................................................... 11

Carrie Bradshaw…or Scary Bradshaw? ......................................... 19

Mistress of the Dark ....................................................................... 23

The Man Who Loved Dogs and Hated People ............................. 27

The Guy Who Left a Turkey at My Doorstep ............................... 33

Bizarre Love Triangle ..................................................................... 37

Don't Write Your Memoirs ............................................................ 41

Mary Ann Singleton Can Suck It ................................................... 51

Silicon Valley of the Dolls .............................................................. 61

You Say Portola, I Say Crapola ...................................................... 67

Suicide Is Not the Answer .............................................................. 69

Bringing Back the Mojo ................................................................. 73

Destiny's Charles ............................................................................ 81

The Butterflies of the Night ........................................................... 87

Time to Invest in Uber ................................................................... 93

The Ride Comes to an End ............................................................ 95

My Acknowledgements .................................................................. 99

# The Mongolian She-Beast

"This woman was unspeakably evil. She totally gets a chapter in my next book. I'm calling her the Mongolian She-Beast!"

"The Mongolian She-Beast? Well, there goes your NAACP Image Award."

"What?"

"What if someone calls you racist?"

My handsome friend's declaration that my title might be less than PC gave me pause for thought. Some of my best friends are Mongolian. OK, that's not true. However, I lived in Japan for 12 years and hold a master's degree in Asian Studies. I'm pretty sure I'm not a Mongolian-hating bigot or an Anti-Mongite or what have you.

But here we are in twenty-first century San Francisco where merely pointing out someone's ethnicity or nationality prods the easily butthurt types to immediately brand one with a scarlet letter "R" for "Racist." So I'm not going to trot out the tired badges of tolerance you might expect: I've had XX number of Asian boyfriends or I have XX number of African American friends. I am merely pointing out that she was A. Mongolian B. a beast. Those two qualifiers are not necessarily linked. Also, as a comedian and writer, I think the phrase "Mongolian She-

Beast" just sounds funny. My apologies to anyone who might believe otherwise in Ulan Bator.

Anyway, this bitch got me fired. I suspect she was a direct descendent of bloodthirsty Mongolian despot Kublai Khan who had somehow found her way to the register at the poor man's Jamba Juice in the Marina. Never had I been fired from a job in my life, and six months after moving to San Francisco, I had gotten the axe twice. The first time came from a canvassing company, because I wasn't making the fundraising quota for political causes ($140 per day in this case). Then the Mongolian She-Beast got me fired from a juice shop.

What the Hell was I doing at a juice shop anyway? I held a postgraduate degree. I had written for *Bazaar*. Let's just say I had been out of work for the most part since returning to the USA, and my time in San Francisco so far had been a complete fiasco. Tired of just sitting around doing nothing, I grabbed a stack of résumés, a list of health food shops, and hit the streets. If I'm going to waste my education at some soul-sucking hourly wage, I might as well do something healthy, I reasoned.

One finally called me back: Juice Guru in the Marina. Yes, Juice Guru was just as douchey as it sounds. The place was run by a ponytailed guy with a salt-and-pepper beard. Despite managing a health food shop, he kept a cigarette behind his ear in case he needed to smoke real quick. He placed Neenga (the Mongolian She-Beast) in charge of my training.

"Princess is gonna do well today? Princess gonna juice fine?" Ponytail said nuzzling Neenga's chin the day I was hired.

She grunted, "Unnn." I don't think she understood what was said, but she understood she held the owner's nutsack in the palm of her claw-like hands.

I began my Saturday morning bright and perky. I was happy just to be useful and not be hemorrhaging money like I had since I arrived in San Francisco. I took out the garbage to a fly-infested compost heap. I washed empty blenders as Neenga served ginger root smoothies and "paninis," which were actually just cheese and ham on toast. Next I cleaned the wheatgrass lint out of the juicer, then mopped. I Purelled the smell away and washed my hands to ready for more happy juicery.

"Do you need some help, Neenga?" I asked her.

She grunted and said "Oog," pointing to the orange juicer.

The machine rather brusquely stripped the oranges of their skins and squeezed the fresh juice out into a pitcher. After twenty or so oranges were juiced, I had a good pitcher full of fresh OJ, but needed to get rid of the rinds the machine precariously tossed in a pail. I picked them up and as they started falling on the floor, I asked Neenga for help.

"Would you help me throw these away please?" The rinds were drippy, and the only trash bin was situated in front of Neenga's crotch.

The floor was getting wet. "Neenga, would you let me throw these out?"

The shop was empty. She looked at me getting sticky, then twirled her hair.

"Would you move please?"

She looked at me, grunted, and moved a step—making my access to the garbage even harder. Her eyes challenged me saying, "How about that?"

"Neenga, I need you to step aside."

"Oog."

"Look you fuckin' juice bitch. You need to get out of the way so I can dispose of these."

"Fuck you."

Oh, now she spoke English.

"Could we please just work together? I just want to get rid of these." A rind fell from my hands.

"Fuck you."

"Look, I'm just trying to work. Why are you making it so hard?"

"Fuck you."

"You say fuck you one more time you juicy jezebel—" I shook an orange rind in her face.

"Fuck you."

She grabbed the shop phone, and ran into the storeroom. How could a storage space filled with strawberries, kiwi fruit and other such pleasantries brew such hatred? I figured the spirulina was infecting her brain.

Ponytail arrived within minutes and even though she had been an amalgam of surly, snarky and cruel, when the manager arrived, she immediately started crying.

"Now this is some bullshit," I muttered as Ponytail took the girl in his arms. She only knew the words "ooog" and "fuck you" in English, but her acting chops were Meryl Streep quality.

"Neenga says you slapped her. You see this camera? It recorded everything you did." He pointed to a small glass eye hidden among some shelves.

"If you look at the footage, you'll see she is insane."

"Is this my shop's shirt?"

"Yes."

"Take it off, and get the fuck out of my shop."

"But, let's watch this video together."

"Leave now and I won't press charges."

"Wait! You don't understand."

"Out!"

I took the shirt off and zipped my blue Adidas hoodie over my bare chest. Now I wanted to cry.

This is when destiny bitch slapped me. There was a large block party up and down the street. Kids bounced about and ate cotton candy. "Daddy, Daddy! I wanna jump in the Moon Walk."

*I gotta get outta here.* Then I remembered I only had one dollar left, and bus fare was $2. I had intended to use tips to get home. I took a ride on the Muni 22 bus anyway. *Fuck this city* I thought as I hid in the back of the bus.

Then I remembered the Marina, a new-ish development of San Francisco, was built on landfill. During the next Big One, this district might be devastated by soil liquefaction. At least when the earthquake comes, Ponytail and the Mongolian She-Beast will be the first to die in the tsunami. Actually, I don't wish people to die. I hope for poetic justice. I wish for them to see me on TV someday and realize what assholes they were when they knew me.

# From Twink to Daddy

Armistead Maupin's *Tales of the City* brought me to San Francisco. Maupin's series was the leavening agent that got my San Francisco cake to rise. All the other ingredients were firmly in place. San Francisco is a city with generally amicable weather and generally amicable people (give or take the occasional She-Beast). The Bay Area as a whole was on the upswing economically, despite the Great Recession. *Tales of the City* factors in because more than any one detail or character, I took with me from the books that San Francisco is a place you could simply arrive and recreate yourself. Also, I had the notion that sexuality, race and gender identity would be a secondary basis of judgment. Hopefully my character would be the primary focus of my interactions with people, rather than external factors. This was not always the case, of course, but in San Francisco you come closer to achieving this ideal than in most places.

As a teen I visited SF to check out colleges, and the first San Francisco gay bar I tried to sneak into was the Café. The doorman sniffed at my fake Iowa driver's license that listed my name as "Nathan Murray," so I scooted down 16th street to Esta Noche, which featured a heavily working class Latino crowd and an all-Spanish drag revue.

I clearly remember during the taxi ride back to my hotel, the 50-something driver with a graying porn-stache hit on me saying, "What do you say I come back in thirty minutes and we feel around?" It was so creepy I remember those words verbatim. What do you say we fucking don't feel around Chester the Molester? I was 17 at the time and looked it. I eventually moved to New York City to attend university, but I filed SF into my mental cabinet as a place I wanted to live in the future. At least I'll have a lot of entertaining taxi rides, I reasoned.

Fast-forward to 2011. I found myself unemployed and burned out after twelve years in Japan and when the March 11 earthquake hit the islands, I returned to the USA. Though I had visited every other year or so and kept up with current events online, the United States had evolved in the twelve years I had been gone. Small, mostly intangible things had shifted. Rap metal died. Comedian Dave Chappelle's zeitgeist had meteorically come and gone. Beards happened. Zombies replaced vampires as the horror menace *du jour*. Rosie O'Donnell had come then gone then come back again. The *Real Housewives* created a legacy of aspirational bourgeois buffoonery.

I was aware of most of these things when I came back from Japan—I was in Tokyo working in media, after all. Tokyo is more plugged in than say the shrub-covered savannahs of Namibia. Though I hear Namibia has some pretty kick-ass Wi-Fi nowadays so they're probably plugged in as well.

If I wanted to see a TV show from the USA, a YouTube clip could just as easily be procured in Japan, which is how I learned about *Glee, Game of Thrones* and *Chelsea Lately*. Japanese cable stations also licensed big American shows such as *Sex and the City* or *American Idol* several months or even years after the original American airdates, but ain't nobody got time for that. If my friends on American social media were all talking about a certain show, I didn't wait around for Fox Japan to license it and finally air it months after the conclusion could already be read about online.

One thing that had certainly changed in the years away is that I had entered into "Daddy-hood." Now in my 30s in the USA, service workers in shops and restaurants all addressed me as "Sir." I call this era "Daddy" not because of any actual paternity on my part. The baby on the cover of this book is a red herring.

I was 33 the first time a younger paramour yelled out, "Give it to me Daddy!" in bed. This guy was in his twenties and not *all that* younger. To sum things up, all this business about Sir and Daddy could be hot. But on the other hand, sometimes it simply made me feel old. I know that kid at Starbucks thinks he's being polite when he says, "Here's your Grande Frappuccino, Sir." But what he is really doing is making me feel elderly. Ancient in fact. Like some Mesopotamian relic that waltzed out of centuries past, wobbling about with my cane and my dentures and yelling at those darn kids to get the fuck off my lawn.

Other cultures demarcate this nebulous age threshold in various ways. French women must eventually vacate the Mademoiselle pedestal to join the ranks of Madames. In days past, in the USA "Miss" would automatically become "Ma'am." Men in Japan eventually grow out of *oni-chan* (older brother) and become addressed as *oji-san* or *o-cchan* (uncle). Though American English at large does not have such a clear cut age-based demarcation, I argue that in the gay community being addressed as "Daddy" signified that I graduated from "twink"—that's gay slang for nubile and hairless young men. But now I had cast off this vestige of youth and became a "Daddy." I am entirely aware that some gays place "Daddy" as somewhat older—like 45 to 50—but like I said 33 was the age someone first told this Daddy to spank him hard, so I'm going to mark my entry into Daddy-dom at 33.

In addition to me becoming a Daddy in a psychological sense, many of the men I knew growing up were now in fact biological Daddies. They had kids. Lots of kids. Even the gay ones had kids. It's as if around 32 the dam burst and babies were the new best thing. Babies were the new black. Babies were the Birken. I had a variety of friends across California from college, but they were abandoning the hedonism of the city and migrating to the sensible suburbs. My entire peer circle and social life was now annihilated by infants. It forced me to find new friends and redefine what I enjoyed doing with my old friends. It made me consider whether my entrenched bachelorhood was a place of liberation—or was I like Carrie Bradshaw, hungover and looking like a swamp monster on the cover of *New York* magazine: Single and Fabulous? That question mark was hostile.

# The Gummy Bear Ghetto

I left Tokyo after the March 11 earthquake that Wikipedia describes as a "Megathrust Earthquake." Though I am highly tempted to write a series of jokes using the word "Megathrust," the reality of the earthquake was not funny at all. I shall digress from humor for a few sentences. Around 15,000 people died in the quake or were swallowed by the tsunami that crashed against the northeastern shore of Japan. Thousands were displaced by the Fukushima nuclear disaster. As I wrote about the experience in my first book, I figured this was an opportune moment to repatriate myself in the Land of the Free and Home of the Brave. So where to move after experiencing an earthquake of historically immense proportions? San Francisco! Just call me the Quake Chaser. For me, earthquakes are like Pokémon. Gotta catch 'em all.

OK, I may be ridiculous, but I'm not quite that ridiculous. Moving to Northern California had a lot to do with the fact that much of my family had gradually wandered over to NorCal from the Midwest. In fact, I have often thought that most Midwesterners secretly dream of living in California—sort of like the Manifest Destiny that we never accomplished. I ponder the lives of my ancestors who traversed great distances from Europe to get to the USA. These people withstood small pox,

Native American threats (either real or perceived), and finally got over to Kansas City where they all basically said, "Fuck it! We are not dealing with all the dysentery, mountain lions and rattlesnakes waiting for us on the Oregon Trail. Seriously, KC is where we are staying." Essentially by reaching California, my family and I have completed the Manifest Destiny of the House of St. Anthony.

I took advantage of my older sister Victoria's kind offer to stay for an extended period with her family in Carmel. In 2011, the US economy was still like a lazy dick in need of Viagra, so the thousands of résumés I sent out in the Carmel area went unnoticed, unloved and untouched.

I realized what an employment black hole I had fallen into. Had I gone back to New York or Los Angeles, there would at least be a few possibilities for Japanese bilingual like me, but unfortunately on this stretch of California coastline, I was out of luck. Carmel was neither here nor there, and even though Carmel is fabulous, it held little opportunity for me then.

A fateful trip awaited me, though. My sister and I made a trip two hours north up to San Francisco for an event called Bring Your Own Big Wheel (or BYOBW). I had visited San Francisco before, but this was the first time I witnessed the type of humor and debauchery San Francisco relishes.

At BYOBW, people dressed in costumes as varied as Amy Winehouse to Captain Caveman. They rode at breakneck speed on children's plastic big wheels down Vermont Street in Potrero Hill.

A Ninja Turtle said "Sorry, bro" as he ran over my foot. A slutty hamster yodeled as she whizzed down the crooked pathway. This was when I found out that in addition to being a city, San Francisco provided year-round excuses for grown-ass adults to dress in costumes and get drunk in public. I love costumes so much I have my drag alter ego, Natasha Foxx, so I was all for this aspect of San Francisco culture. I could run boozed up and naked for Bay to Breakers or in red and white undies at the Santa Claus-inspired Santa Skivvies Race. Folsom Street Fair (leather festival) and Dore Alley (more of the same) provided a place for the leather harnesses gathering dust in my closet. Although I mention Folsom and Dore Alley, I will admit I'm not a hardcore leather Daddy. I'm more like leather LITE—I'm content to shimmy about in public in a latex jock strap or get spanked a couple times. Shit like electric nipple torture and hardcore fist-fucking I'll leave to the more adventurous.

The undeniable scene of San Francisco led me to make a snap decision. I dusted off my old copy of *Tales of the City*, packed a suitcase, and left on the next bus out of Carmel in search of my own Madrigal House. The Madrigal House, for those unfamiliar with the *Tales of the City* series, is the welcoming abode where protagonist Mary Ann Singleton lives when she packs up and moves from Ohio to San Francisco. Would my own Madrigal House filled with gays and hippies await me as I launched my life in the city by the Bay?

My arrival in San Francisco was not nearly as exciting as Bring Your Own Big Wheel. I disembarked the bus in the Financial District surrounded by skyscrapers. Literally zero people were on the streets on this Sunday evening, save a smattering of tourists dawdling about by the Ferry Building.

"Where is everybody?" I'm sure I heard an echo. "Body… body… body? Is anybody home… home… home…?" This is how I learned that parts of downtown were absolutely empty on the weekends—except for a few homeless vagrants and some elderly Asian women with push carts who rifled through the garbage bins on the streets.

I took a cab to the Upper Haight where a friend of the family hosted me. She lived with her tech-employed boyfriend and she described the near death-grip monopoly Craigslist presently holds over the local renters market.

"If you find a place, show up with your checkbook in your hand or it will probably get rented that day by someone else," she described the competitive landscape.

The first landlord I spoke with in bourgeois Noe Valley required five references, a note from my mother, a $10,000 deposit, the kiss from an angel (preferably archangel Gabriel), the teardrop of a heartbroken minotaur and 17 months of rent deposit in cash up front. And I needed to already have a job.

The next place I contacted asked me to visit—Thomas Avenue. The cab driver looked at me funny when I gave him the address. "Do you have any way to get back from there? I don't drive to the Bayview District at night." Unlike the areas teeming with the gays and hippies that I imagined, parts of the City were straight up hood.

Some of the less savory areas of the city, while gentrifying rapidly, sound so delightful on paper. The Tenderloin, affectionately known as the TL, makes me real hungry for a Tri-tip Steak Sandwich. Then you have "Bayview" and "Visitacion Valley," which sound like sweet retirement homes—like you go there and "Moon River" is playing while jolly senior citizens eat cheesecake and play shuffleboard.

However, looking at the online crime maps of San Francisco, these are places to use your street smarts and be wary of. I personally have never encountered trouble in any of these areas, and the TL boasts some of the coolest bars and restaurants in the City. You might have to hopscotch over human feces on the sidewalk or avoid some persistent OxyContin dealers on the way, but trendy and dodgy often come hand in hand.

The next apartment I visited was actually in the TL, and I wondered why the drug dealers kept saying "Cheez-Its"—was this a new drug? Like the kids today are taking Molly with a side of Cheez-Its? Is it a cocaine laced snack cracker or something? It turns out what I heard as "Cheez-Its" was actually "Chiva," a street term for heroin.

After a couple intense days of contacting rooms throughout the city, a Filipino gentleman offered me the chance to rent a room in a house in Ingleside. This misty section of town near City College is sort of like a million dollar ghetto—the area situates at the southernmost part of San Francisco next to Daly City. At time of writing, the houses of Ingleside average a mere $630,000, which is a steal compared to the city-wide average of $1.52 million per home.

The houses on my street featured brightly colored façades that reminded me of Gummy Bear colors. Along Ocean Avenue, there was a gym and a few grocery stores, but what really sold me on the area was that a psychic along the street had a big neon sign that said "Plam Reading" with the word "Palm" misspelled. Considering it takes a while to create a neon sign, couldn't the psychic have seen this problem coming? If this is how people half-ass things in this neighborhood, this is the place for me. The irony is that "Palm" being misspelled got lots of attention, so people would stop and gawk at the sign and take photos for Instagram.

Ingleside is mostly safe. I say mostly because in the time I was there, the Chinese mafia put out a hit on a family a block away—which made the news for its "quintuple homicide" (that means they killed five people). Another night, I heard what I thought were firecrackers before realizing the sounds were gun shots. These shots led to the death of a young man in the neighborhood, again putting Ingleside in the news for all the wrong reasons.

The McDonald's along Ocean Avenue could be counted on for dicey entertainment value. There is a fenced off area, which I imagine used to house a McDonald's-themed playground. However, thugs could be seen there smoking the good stuff at any time during the day. I suppose the McDonald's staff took all the playground fixtures away, as you can't have panhandlers straddling Birdy the Early Bird while gangsters paint graffiti on Mayor McCheese. Shit's about to go down if you play in the ball cage and don't proffer the hobos some McNuggets.

I try not to go there, but once I intensely craved a chocolate shake. Of course when I sat down, a man with a teardrop tattoo seated himself next to me while I was busy reading celebrity gossip via Dlisted on my iPhone.

"Can I use your phone?"

"Sir, no one may use my phone."

"Ah, man. Just need to make a local call."

"I don't care if you are making a direct call to Mother Theresa in heaven to pray for food to feed orphaned kittens of the Sudan. No one may use my phone."

"Damn. Just trying to make a phone call. Help a brother out."

My sassiness might have been ill-advised considering a tear drop tattoo often indicates time served for murder, but I would not budge.

"Sir, no one may use my phone. The only people who use my phone also whisper sweet nothings in my ear and take me to a classy dinner at Olive Garden. I think their breadsticks are indicative of true love. Are you prepared to do that?"

The man left.

# Carrie Bradshaw...or Scary Bradshaw?

Another reason I chose to move to SF was that it offered a larger pool of gay bachelors my age, and I had my sights set on gettin' hitched. In fact, San Francisco is a veritable Lake Superior of a dating pool for gay men aged thirty and up. While I imagine the scenes of New York or LA are twinkier and glossier, San Francisco seemed less inclined to make me feel like I was Methuselah shaking my walker at flocks of hairless, squealing 20-year-old Adonises (Adonii?). Because after 30, age crept on me. A man's body makes thirty-something smells and sprouts hair in thirty-something places. Ear hair waxing was added to my beauty regimen. I recently had to pluck a grey nose hair.

I lamented these changes to an African American drag queen friend. "My twenties were about Grey Goose, and now my thirties are about grey nose hair?"

Girlfriend schooled me saying, "Bitch, you ain't a little twink anymore. You're a grown ass man now."

I loved the bar scenes in SoMa (South of Market) and Castro, but I tried to expand the sites of my social connections to make different types of friends. Though the bars were there when I wanted to put in a cameo, I volunteered at a hotline for

LGBT people (or LGBTQQIA to be extra inclusive), and I knew various extracurriculars were readily available. Any American city of a certain size has a gay softball team, but San Francisco also offers a gay swim team, gay martial arts, gay knitting, and even gay windsurfing. If I did feel like indulging in the bar scene, my Ground Zero would be the Midnight Sun, where I could have a beer and a flirt while watching viewings of shows such as *True Blood* or *RuPaul's Drag Race*.

One thing I immediately noticed about San Francisco's scene when I arrived was that all the men had facial hair. There are several factors that made face follicles mandatory in that day and age. This was the height of the Brian Wilson "Fear the Beard" zeitgeist, as the Giants had just won the World Series in 2010. On top of this, San Francisco's leather scene encourages facial hair as it can make any screaming queen appear wildly masculine—at least we appear masculine until we open our mouths and Tinkerbell comes flying out. Also, San Francisco is always kinda cold, so increased fuzziness helps increase heat.

Not that every beard I saw was sexy. If your beard looks like Rutherford B. Hayes, Ulysses S. Grant or any President from the nineteenth century United States, I won't be putting out. Santa Claus is not a fuckable look either. Don't even get me started at the hideous mustache wax business amongst the hipsters that looks like the Lyft logo. Sorry, but I shall not be dating anyone that looks like Cap'n Crunch. For that matter anyone that looks like a cereal logo is out: neither Toucan Sam,

Lucky the Leprechaun, Count Chocula, nor Frankenberry. Only Tony the Tiger can get it.

At any rate, most of the hottest guys had facial hair when I arrived in 2011, so I decided to try it out. And the beard worked. In fact it *really* worked. Hitherto in my 33 years on planet earth, the best compliment I would generally get was "cute," but the closer I started looking to Barba Papa, the more guys started telling me I was "sexy." I find it odd that it took 33 years to finally find a look that others found sexy, but I'll take it from where I can get it.

Given my new beard infused charisma, I set out in search of my prince. I've definitely kissed a few frogs along the way. Or maybe I'm just slutty. Sometimes I felt my husband search was taking a little too long. As if my *Sex in the City* style manhunt was racking up higher numbers than I'd like to admit. Then I had some outright terrifying dating experiences, which made me start wondering, "Am I Carrie Bradshaw…or Scary Bradshaw?" Here are some the highlights and lowlights in my dating fiesta!

# Mistress of the Dark

I met Lamont at Bar 440 the first month I arrived in San Francisco. Feeling drunk with power from my sexy beard, I zeroed right in on him since Lamont was dark, swarthy and covered in a sexy tattoo sleeve. We briefly flirted and debated important topics such as who was better: Lil' Kim or Nicki Minaj. Lamont flagged down a taxi to my home approximately eight minutes later. We made out in the back seat while enjoying the Best Hits of Afghanistan that the taxi driver had on his CD player.

Fireworks! Chandelier swinging! Wolves howling! The night was long and the heat was intense, so I was disappointed when I didn't hear from Lamont again.

Four months later, I ran into him at the Midnight Sun during a *Project Runway* viewing night, and we had a repeat performance. Then again a couple months later we did the same and so on. I resigned myself to the fact that this was just a semi-casual hookup situation.

I was fine with this, but what bothered me the most was that he always insisted in coming over to my shitty place—which wasn't exactly the Ritz-Carlton. It was a glorified closet behind the garage in a house of the Gummy Bear Ghetto, and when we woke up, my elderly Filipino housemates would usually be having a heated argument in Tagalog while cooking this smelly-ass fish that made the whole place stink like a chewed-up dog toy. OK, I guess it wasn't a huge surprise Lamont never wanted to date me, but this room was $500 a month and near the BART station. I needed to hold onto it as long as possible. But why didn't Lamont just have me over to his place? Was he living in a pigsty? Did he have a live-in lover?

The mystery of Lamont's place was solved when I ran into him on Diamond Street outside Glen Park Station.

"Hey Charles."

"What's good, Boss?"

"You looking good."

"I'm working on my fitness, Lamont.'

"Is that working or werking?"

"That's for me to know and you to find out."

"Let's go find out then."

He lived around the corner, and he told me to make myself comfortable while he went in the other room and freshened himself up.

"I'll be back in two shakes of a lamb's tail," Lamont said. He scampered off while I watched a *South Park* rerun on his flat screen. I admired the slightly Gothic décor that added a dramatic flair to the proceedings. The *South Park* characters made jokes about AIDS and herpes. I remember feeling uneasy, as the last things you want to think about just before you go fuck someone are a couple of incurable STIs.

"Let me give you the tour," Lamont said. He showed me the dining room and den area. Then he took me into a closet-like alcove. In his man-cave, I saw a large Pentagram on the ground, a Wiccan alter, and various pictures of Elvira, Mistress of the Dark. There were pictures of Lamont with Elvira, beaming. Her boobies looked camera-perfect. Up above all this Gothic insanity hung multiple models of the Star Trek Enterprise and other sci-fi bric-a-brac.

*So this is why he never has invited me over.*

I personally am not scared of Wicca, since I think there is wisdom to be found in every type of spirituality. Still, the Pentagram, the shrine to Elvira, and the Trekkie Extravaganza overhead was a lot to process. I liked the intensity of his hobbies, though. Being around someone this passionate about his interests turned me on.

"Throw me into the bedroom, Prince of Darkness!"

"Yes, Daddy."

"Ravage my body."

"Woof!"

"Grrr!"

For the uninitiated, making animal noises is a perfectly legitimate form of communication among gay men nowadays, as we also call each other otters, cubs, bears, silver bears, pandas and so on; each animal refers to different attributes, such as body type. For example, a bear is generally a hairy man with more meat than a cub. Silver bears tend to be older. Anyway, the animal heat was in full-effect for this moment with Lamont. If I had to choose, I'd say he was a wolverine and I was a capybara. I don't even know what that means, but I'm sure we should have made some animal noises.

I see him on occasion and we'll have a chat in the Castro or on Facebook. Maybe after running into him over drinks at the Midnight Sun sometime I can drag him home to role play "Captain Jean-Luc Picard manhandles Dr. Beverly Crusher." As long as he goes full Klingon on my ass and my Filipino housemates don't cook that smelly fish again, I'll be happy.

# The Man Who Loved Dogs and Hated People

After cruising me in the 24 Hour Fitness sauna, Samson followed me outside. I personally prefer to date guys near my age so they get my *Thundercats* jokes and references to Lady Kier from Deee-Lite. Samson was a good twenty years my senior, but he had a rock-hard body, so I thought I'd try something new and give this older dude a chance.

He invited me back to his place with a pool in Silicon Valley.

I admitted to him that during my teen years, I didn't quite grasp that Silicon Valley was basically a bunch of sleepy suburbs that house a battalion of powerful tech companies. Back in high school, I thought Silicon Valley was actually a place in the countryside where people mined silicon ore to make computer chips. If you're actually working for Apple or researching at Stanford it's all pretty exciting, but outside these places, Silicon Valley is mostly residential and has a lot of strip malls and car dealerships.

Anyway, Samson drove us in his Tesla to his condo in Redwood City. I made myself at home while he frolicked with his ugly, smelly dog.

"Harley! Hey Harley! How you doing Harley?" He let the dog lick his face and pet the animal so hard that I doubt Harley enjoyed it. His attention to Harley verged on inappropriate, as he gave Harley's nutsack a swift whack.

Personally, I have nothing against dogs. I quite like clean and well-behaved dogs. However, dog owners, especially on the West Coast, embrace a sense of entitlement that's truly grating. I'm not as excited about dogs as their owners seem to think I should be. I call the animals OPDs: Other People's Dogs. I don't want OPDs in my grocery store. I don't want OPDs in my bed. I don't need to see more than a couple pictures of OPDs in my Facebook feed.

Not all dog owners are this bad. I just hate the ones that go around walking their dog with a dog-shit-eating grin on their face while obviously using their animal to fish for attention. It's like, "Yeah, we got it. Your Dalmatian is amazing. You're still a fucking dumb ass, though."

Samson was a buffoon because not only did he psychologically project all these positive attributes to his dog, but he also scapegoated humans for all that was wrong in his life. He was kind of a dick to other homo sapiens.

I figured I couldn't write off a guy just because of his dog. Valentine's Day was a week away and spending that holiday alone always sucks. Every guy has a certain foible, *n'est-ce pas*? So I didn't make a big deal about the asshole Samson became when he was around his dog.

What scared me more was the way he treated other people. One night we kept trying to get HBO Go to work on his cable, but the internet was off and the loading icon started spinning around and around like a dreidel on a particularly festive night of Hanukkah. "I have to call the cable company again," he said lovingly, patting Harley.

He called his provider. I felt shocked at the vitriol in his voice as the man who had just been fondling his dog's head turned into Regan from *The Exorcist*. I could hear the Indian guy's voice trembling as Samson launched into a tirade about how his Internet providers were a bunch of disgusting road whores and he was going to catch the next flight to their call center in India and beat the crap out of everyone if we couldn't watch *Game of Thrones* in the next few minutes.

After berating the poor Indian telecom worker, we switched his Internet box off then on again, and were soon using HBO Go with no problem. I imagined that as a kid, Samson must have been one of those children who got too excited playing *The Legend of Zelda* and would throw his controller at the Nintendo console if Link died.

On our next date, he offered to take me to a Korean restaurant which really is the way to my heart since I love meat and spicy food. But then he brought Harley with us and even put a little sweater on Harley as we went outside. I wasn't going to say anything because Samson was paying, but the other patrons kept giving us the stink eye as he fed Harley expensive *bulgogi* right off the table.

"This is sure good stuff," he said to the server. "It better not be dog meat!" I turned bright red as the kimchee on the table. "Where's our fortune cookie?"

*This guy is a either ignorant or completely racist,* I thought as he kissed his dog at the table. Then I clenched my teeth together when I noticed he left a three dollar tip on a sixty dollar tab. The former restaurant employee in me was mortified. I slipped a twenty dollar bill onto the table as Samson and Harley went to the parking lot to get his Tesla.

I was really ready to dump Samson at this point, but Valentine's Day was two days away and he kept saying he was going to take me to the Michelin-rated French Laundry and buy me this shirt I really wanted from Prada Sport. Then Valentine's Day arrived and nothing. Tumbleweeds. By 9 p.m. I realized nothing was happening that night, so my date for Valentine's 2012 was a bottle of Smirnoff and Billie Holiday.

I was livid, simply because he had talked this moment up for so long and completely flaked on me. The next week, I called him and said I thought I deserved to know what went wrong.

"No chemistry. You leave me cold."

This mystified me as he always seemed ready and eager to have sex multiple times per visit. I was incensed that he disposed of me like a used paper plate. I'm sure he was just fobbing me off as we reached that "time to commit" juncture in a dating cycle. No wonder he was 53 and still living alone with his ugly dog.

"Yeah, well you're old and your dog is annoying." I'm really not proud I said this.

"How could you say something so insensitive? I never knew you were that mean. What Harley? Yes, Harley, Daddy is here." I heard the dog licking his face.

# The Guy Who Left a Turkey at My Doorstep

Kevin worked at a sandwich shop, and hit on me while I really just wanted some pulled pork. He kept flirting as he made my sandwich, and I resisted.

"Hey you're pretty cute."

"Can I get my bread toasted?"

"Maybe we should hang out sometime?"

"Can I get the pulled pork to go?" I told the blonde cutie. I stifled the jokes going through my head about him pulling my pork.

"Here's my number." He handed it to me with the pulled pork and BBQ Lays. I fished for some quarters to put in the jar that said, "Sexy People Tip." Then I looked at him. He had this really dumb grin and sapphire blue eyes that pleaded with me in just in the right way. The Silicon Valley shakedown with Samson had just happened, so he caught me at a weak moment.

We headed over to Two Dollar Tuesdays at 440 Castro, and after a few Lagunitas and laughs, I warmed up to Kevin. His soul patch belonged in 1992 and his come-ons were cheesy, but I found it endearing. Also, he didn't have an intense relationship with any dogs that I knew of. At least I'll never go wanting for Black Forest Ham or Philly Cheesesteak I reasoned. Our courtship felt very juvenile as he would bring a six pack of Sierra Nevada over, we'd have a laugh and watch whatever stupid viral videos were up on YouTube and make out.

A couple nights after we met, he said he'd come over after work and cook me something. I said OK and waited. I waited for hours. I had conquered most of the world on my *Civilization* game on my phone, when I gave up at 3 a.m. and went to bed. He wasn't answering the phone, and I was tired, angry, and hungry.

I went to get my morning latte the next day and to my surprise, a Thanksgiving-sized turkey was in the doorway of our house as I exited. The turkey, still in its wrapper, was wet from the dewy San Francisco night air. Apparently, Kevin had traipsed over stoned in the middle of the night. Because his phone had died, he repeatedly rang the doorbell that went to the rooms above me. He woke up all the Filipino people who thought he was some crazy person ringing the doorbell at 4 a.m. Kevin left the turkey in the doorway and pranced off into the night.

"Mabuhay!" I cheerily greeted the Filipinos as I carried the giant turkey to my room at 8 a.m.

Kevin called later to say, "Wanna smoke some pot?" He apologized for getting me in trouble with my roommates.

I was irked. Flaking out was one thing, but putting my reasonably priced San Francisco accommodations in jeopardy was quite another.

"You know, I'm a little busy right now. Try me later," I begged off, then went to the library to chill out.

I got home, turned on my phone, and there were no less than sixteen messages from Kevin, each with greater and greater reaches of hysteria.

"Hi Charles, this is Kevin. Babe I'm really into you. I'm sorry about—" delete.

"Charles, this is Kevin. You're my prince charming—" delete.

"Charles. I don't appreciate it. I put all my love into that pulled pork. Stop blocking my calls—" delete.

"Babe! BABE! How can we get married if—" delete delete delete delete.

I knew that with my sexy beard that guys were more into me, but who thought this turkey-wielding sandwich artist would get dickmatized so thoroughly? In fact, I hadn't been blocking his calls before, but realized that blocking him was an extremely good idea.

# Bizarre Love Triangle

One of the reasons people love the bubble of San Francisco is that people are so liberal here—things that are normal aren't necessarily normal anywhere else. Three staples of liberal sexual mores that immediately come to mind for me are 1. The empowered Trans community 2. The prevalence of faux queens 3. The normalcy of polyamory. To elaborate, my Trans friends who felt alienated when they lived elsewhere usually say they are more at ease in San Francisco. They still encounter transphobia at times, but not to the degree they faced in whatever Godforsaken fiefdom they hailed from. Also, *faux queens* are a thing here—that's a woman who loves to dress up extravagantly like a drag queen. Faux queens are women pretending to be men dressed as women. A faux queen who performs with the name Ferosha Titties is a nightlife staple about SF. Finally, polyamory is commonplace here. For example, lots of gay men form *triads* in San Francisco. Honey, you don't have to worry about sexual orientation in the City. You have to worry about sexual *disorientation*!

I met "the couple" on Independence Day several seasons ago, and they hunted me like a couple of hammerhead sharks circling a baby seal. One approached me to chat while the other bought me drinks. I usually don't really play hard to get—in fact,

I'm pretty much a sure thing. So the hammerheads got their lunch and whole lot more. One of them was a refugee from Sri Lanka who had fled his homeland during a period of crisis, and the other was his social worker who happened to be independently wealthy. The social worker had helped the refugee acclimate to the United States, and they had fallen in love while filling out green card applications. Together they owned a palatial residence in Pac Heights near the stone mansion occupied by romance author Danielle Steele.

The couple had been together more than a decade, and this wasn't their first visit to the Island of the Triads. These guys were in their forties, so I was comparatively younger—I brought a freshness to their marriage while they looked after me and took me out.

The most remarkable thing about the triad was how unremarkable it was. In fact, it was possibly the healthiest relationship I'd had in years. If you can get over your jealousy, then an arrangement like this was loads of fun. I had two handsome men showering me with attention, buying me delicious dinners and taking me to shows. In return, I cooked for them sometimes and kept the proceedings lively. This helped me get out of my funk as I was unemployed at this time. We would go out, have a laugh, eat gorgeous nomnoms, then all go back to their mansion and fuck the daylights out of each other.

My only worry was that after triad, what exactly do you have to do to make things even *more* exciting? Once a *ménage à trois* is no longer special and just another thing you do, what exactly is next? Make love while sniffing glue and parachuting down into the Grand Canyon? Jack off an entire NBA basketball team sliding around in baby oil while Roman candles shoot out of your asshole?

I didn't worry too much about that and enjoyed the triad for as long as it lasted. Things between us finally solidified when they programmed the third spot on their car radio to my favorite station.

A triad only works if people can keep their jealousy in check. With the couple, we fulfilled different needs and desires for one another. It was a fairly smooth division of labor. But then it happened.

I had cooked for them and made them drinks all afternoon, and we had plans to go out that night. Then the couple broke plans and ditched me to go play with *another* third. The two of them together I loved, but my inner Glenn Close kicked in with wild-eyed, foaming at the mouth, rabid, jealousy like in *Fatal Attraction*. I was fine with being a third, but like Hell was I going to suffer the insult of being their fourth! So I boiled their pet rabbit and burned all their Mr. S Leather jockstraps in a giant bonfire. "You shall rue the day you met me, you insufferable couple." I rubbed my hands together while I set fire to their Dolce & Gabbana jeans in their BMW like in *Waiting to Exhale*.

Their collection of cock rings turned into the charred remnants of a napalm explosion.

Just kidding. I didn't do anything like that.

The night they decided to ditch me, they dropped me off at a leather bar and gave me twenty dollars. I saw my life fast-forward thirty years with them married and me renting a place alone. Still basically single and unstable. And them still living together with no real intention of being there for me when things got rocky in life. Here I was being left on my own on a normal Saturday night. What would happen on Thanksgiving? And Christmas? And worst of all Halloween?

It was partially my fault for being so needy and oblivious to the basic tenets of polyamory: i.e. that people are free to do as they like as long as certain boundaries are abided to. Anyway, I moved on and they moved on, and much like the Triforce in *The Legend of Zelda* (many of life's lessons can be found in Zelda), we were scattered to the three corners of San Francisco. Or, I scattered to my corner, and they stayed put in their mansion.

# Don't Write Your Memoirs

Or at least consider turning them into a novel before you try publishing. And here's why.

I consider my readers to be the most fabulous, creative, intelligent, urbane residents of planet Earth. Possibly writing a book is a dream that you have considered yourself—it's a fairly common dream. So hopefully you can learn from the drudgery I experienced and reach that dream. Consider carefully, though, whether you wish to publish as fiction or non-fiction. Due to the litigious nature of modern daily life, your non-fiction memoir could easily end up looking like fiction. That is if it ever gets properly published. Read on if you dare!

Unless you have substantial publishing connections or a media following in place, publishing your memoirs can be a harrowing experience—akin to being chased by the Headless Horseman like Ichabod Crane in "The Legend of Sleepy Hollow." Everyone has a story to tell, and there is a glut of memoirs on the market. Publishing houses see memoirs created by an unknown writer as about appealing as a freshly laid dog turd.

First let's look at the state of the publishing industry. I remember when I saw one of the last Border's bookstores closing down in San Francisco. *The Shania Twain Story* and *Uncharted TerriTORI* by Tori Spelling were the last books left in the memoir section of the final clearance sale. If not the worst books, they were the least suited to that marketplace—and publishing is a business. Are you as famous as Tori Spelling or five time Grammy award winner Shania Twain? If yes, then have your management call Simon & Schuster forthwith and get your multi-million dollar book deal. If you are not as famous as them—as in you don't have a national following or major contacts at media outlets—consider fictionalizing your memoirs so that they are a novel. Basically what I am trying to say is that it is really fucking hard to publish memoirs without a major platform already in place and also due to various legal reasons as well.

Publishing my first memoir *Impossibly Glamorous* as paperback and eBook took six years to complete. It originally wasn't meant to be a book, but after realizing that people outside my immediate circle of friends found my stories funny and enlightening, I wrote my book during one of my periods of unemployment (I was unemployed for large portions of 2009 and 2011). I got a copy of *Writer's Market*—a compendium of all things publishing—and shopped around my manuscript I spent years writing.

I sent *Impossibly Glamorous* to agents who specialize in memoirs. I sent it to agents who specialize in LGBT and travel. I sent it to agents who specialize in LGBT travel memoirs. Not only agents, I sent it directly to publishing houses as well: Simon & Schuster, Random House, Penguin Books, Kodansha International, Simon and Garfunkel. I sent my manuscript to everyone I could think of. And their mother. And their cousin. And their cousin's aesthetician that once gave David Sedaris an eyebrow wax.

No. Zero. No market. Not an enticing pitch. Not a good fit. No place in the business. Pack up your typewriter. NADA.

Basically everyone told me my book was worthless piece of publishing dingleberry that no one would ever touch. They told me I was not a special snowflake. You helped interview Stevie Wonder in Japan? You appeared on a bunch of famous TV and radio shows in Asia? Who cares? Writers like Charles are a dime a dozen. *Impossibly Glamorous*? More like just impossible. So everyone in publishing told me I was a nobody without a story to tell. Looking at the memoir section of a bookstore I was 100% certain my book was one thousand times more edifying than *Confessions of an Heiress* by Paris Hilton, but apparently that was the sort of thing people wanted. People like Hilton had a national platform, and it was a bitter pill to swallow.

One of the times I felt closest to breaking into mainstream publishing, I got Augusten Burrough's agent who had helped publish *Running with Scissors* to look at my book. He instilled in me that I was funny and should keep writing, but I should build my own platform: a blog, a podcast, a tap dance revue, a channel on X-Tube, a sitcom, a hotel dynasty. Anything as long as I had a platform to work from and promote my work. Just being fabulous and interesting was not enough to get a book deal—I needed a platform to maintain an audience *and then* maybe I had a chance. "Keep writing," said Burroughs's agent. Then he rejected me.

Later I read an excellent article on self-publishing by Amanda Hocking. She is one of the premier publishing stars of a genre I absolutely detest: young adult fantasy. She discussed how she had gone from an independently published writer to having national book deals. I'm not going to reiterate the entire article, but I realized that A. independent publishing and eBooks were now a viable source of income and B. creating my own path forward rather than waiting for someone to make it for me might be best. Including the time I spent writing and shopping the book around the publishing world, at this point I had already spent four years working on *Impossibly Glamorous*. I wanted to move on with my life. Like many creative people, I had another ten thousand ideas bouncing around my head and I wanted to get started on them.

I finished a draft of *Impossibly Glamorous* in my first months of moving to San Francisco, and I used an ad on Craigslist to discover flame-haired beauty and editor to the stars Marcella Hammer. She welded, sawed, hacked, and polished my book into shape and I released it for the first time on Amazon Kindle in June 2011.

The earth did not move, and I was not suddenly wealthy. In fact, I still could barely get a Deluxe Bacon and Cheese Whopper from Burger King, but the first eBook edition was well-received. Thus I decided to release it as paperback, which I did with assistance from an indie publisher called Fearless Books. They agreed to help me polish up *Impossibly Glamorous* and get it on Ingram's database, which is necessary if you want bookstores to actually buy your book.

We spent months revising and tweaking the text, designing the cover, registering the book with the Library of Congress and the copyright office. Five and a half years had passed since I started on this road, and I was sick of revising *Impossibly Glamorous*. I had to relive all the shittiest things that ever happened to me every time I opened the manuscript. Since those dramatic, tense, and heartbreaking moments are part of a juicy memoir, I had to return to those moments every night in front of my computer. And when I think we're done and I'm so sick of *Impossibly Glamorous* I want to puke all over my Toshiba touchscreen Chromebook, my collaborators at Fearless sent me a very frank email: "Get a lawyer," they said. "Cover your ass."

From a reader's point of view, this version of the book probably would have been a lot more fun. It contained more of the very things that can get you into trouble: sex, drugs, and rock 'n' roll. From a publisher's perspective, these things were also a bonanza of liability. I'm not completely stupid. I had considered some of these things already. The original eBook already changed the names of everyone involved—unless they were a public figure such as Beyoncé or Stevie Wonder. The lawyer I ended up working with told me I could be accused of a plethora of crimes such as violation of privacy, libel, and questionable taste. Then the attorney and I discussed a litany of other copyright questions because in this day and age, people are so greedy that anyone who farts into a microphone thinks they can copyright flatulence. I realized at this late stage that in addition to marketability and talent, these legal factors possibly weighed in on the agents' and publishers' minds when they rejected me five years ago. I'm guessing the agents I sent my original manuscripts thought, "This guy was famous in Japan. OK, that's interesting, but he has no following in the USA, and *Impossibly Glamorous* has way too many liability factors. REJECTED!"

So while I admit my first book is still deliciously juicy (and available for sale on Amazon, Barnes & Noble's website and just about everywhere), the book could have been a WHOLE LOT JUICIER!

I really did strive to be ethical while writing and stay true to my readers, but it was a challenge to have to go back to the text and alter things so that the content of my book did not violate someone's right to privacy. Did changing someone's name… or ethnicity… or species affect the story? Do the messages I wish to convey still hit home? Do I want to contact this person and have them sign a release? Do I never speak to this motherfucker again and let them drift away into the ether? Since the lawyer encouraged me to get releases signed from EVERYONE, if I wanted to keep the story close to reality, I had to have many awkward conversations with people from my past.

Thankfully Facebook has made it extremely easy to find anyone from my distant past, even people I openly detest. Believe me, I had to go through conversations like, "Hey Zachary. I know we haven't seen each other since I spit on you at the 4 Non Blondes featuring Beck concert back in 1993, but would you sign this release for me? How is work at the gas station going? I'm doing well thank you. I'm merely interested in making boatloads of money from royalties once people read and have a laugh at the premature death of our teenage romance. No, I'm not giving you any money."

Then FINALLY on Thanksgiving of 2012, the paperback came out. Just before the Mayan Prophecy that everyone was so scared of turned out to be a giant bucket of horse shit, *Impossibly Glamorous* dispersed throughout the world and everyone loved it. This slim volume of 200-ish pages took six years. Six. Fucking. Years. *Impossibly Glamorous* took longer than it took to conquer Afghanistan. *Impossibly Glamorous* took longer than the American Civil War. *Impossibly Glamorous* took approximately the same amount of time as it took to build the first Transcontinental Railroad—1,907 miles long mind you. *Impossibly Glamorous* took longer than it took to create Mt. Rushmore. Actually, Mt. Rushmore took fourteen years to complete so that's not true! But still this was a long-ass chunk of my life devoted to a book. I could have gotten a PhD. Or six-pack abs. Or a husband.

But the book was what I wanted, and I am 200% satisfied with the result: beautifully designed, professional typography, edited within an inch of its life. Finally the world would know my story! And jellis haterz can kiss my taint, because it's even in San Francisco Public Library and the Library of Congress. I was elated, ecstatic. Not even on Cloud 9, I was on Cloud 99. Several people were unhappy about the book, though.

"What about the time we ate snow cones in third grade?" my cousin Mandy wondered. "Those were, like, some really awesome snow cones. Why isn't that in your book?" Some people had an odd idea of what experiences were noteworthy enough to be in the book. Of course I remember the fucking snow cones, but if something was merely enjoyable, that doesn't make it worth writing about. If I tripped and shoved a snow cone up Mandy's butt, that might have made a funny vignette, but some people just didn't understand what makes for entertaining writing.

My book was marketed to gay men and women roughly between the ages of twenty and fifty. People well outside the target audience read it as well to varying degrees of interest.

"That book was really bawdy," lamented Grandma Betty. Keep in mind if you are going to write a book about sex, partying and rock 'n' roll, even your grandparents will be able to read it once it comes out. I'm rather proud that Grandma Betty thought my book was bawdy—considering she was married four times, one would assume she had extensive experience in the boudoir. It's like a trampy medal of honor or the Hoochie Mama's Purple Heart to be branded bawdy by a woman of such questionable virtue as my beloved grandmother.

This wasn't the first time my creative output had created a public backlash, and my skin has grown fairly thick since I appeared quite often on Japanese TV. The People of the Internet had already called me ugly, fascist, stupid, weird, and grotesque. Which is like totally rude, because I'm definitely not a fascist. One commenter on a popular news website known as Japan Today thought they were insulting me saying I looked like Annie Lennox, but I think that is one of the best compliments I could ever receive.

Then shit happened that freaked me out. It came to my attention some man wrote in a blog post that he knew me when I was sixteen from a teenage gay club, which was odd because I didn't remember him. I checked our mutual acquaintances on Facebook, so I guess it made sense. But I did the math and the guy was like 26 and sneaking into a club for teenyboppers. What's that in the distance? Do I hear an Amber Alert?

Then he wrote on his blog that none of things I wrote about were true and that I was a "wallflower" and a loser. Considering I flounced about on stage in Japan dressed as a slutty dominatrix drag queen, being dissed as a wallflower was entirely new to me. Refreshing almost. I suppose what creeped me out the most was that this person who had no qualms digitally slandering me had been grinding this axe for twenty years. He was so pressed that he has to write about it on his Geocities website for salty old homos or whatever. And like most of my detractors, he hadn't read my book either. The irony is that I had spent six years creating a record of something that my biggest detractors just said was fiction anyway!

So here I propose to you dear reader: if you are thinking of writing a book and might spend six fucking years trying to create a memoir to enlighten and entertain the people of the world only to be dissed, harassed, and called a liar, why not just write a fiction? I believe fiction is easier to get published, and it's easier for movie studios to option to become a film because it requires less legal shucking and jiving. It's probably a lot more lucrative. Just ask J.K. Rowling. Or Dan Brown. Or Amanda Hocking.

and a master's degree, and for stretches of time I had been forced to take several positions that I can only politely describe as well below my skill set.

Play your cards right and the San Francisco dream is yours. Play them wrong, and you'll wind up at a Jamba Juice knockoff trying to fight off the Mongolian She-Beast.

A common issue is that you move to San Francisco only to have your only job prospects open up in the South Bay. You'll have the Hell commute down to the economic engine of Silicon Valley. Of course you can always pay an exorbitant rent to live in the cultural desert that is San Jose, but did you really move to the Bay to live where most people just go home and watch Netflix at night? No, I'm guessing you wanted to live somewhere "happening." Seriously, honey, you might as well stay in Tulsa—at least you'll still have three bedrooms there.

Previously as a Japanese-speaking bilingual American in Tokyo, I never spent any time completely unemployed. Even if I didn't have an office job, I'd have side translation gigs and radio appearances. Moving back after the Fukushima nuclear disaster, the USA was still mired in recession. I moved to San Francisco because I believed, like Mary Ann, that somehow things would just work themselves out.

For the first year I was in SF, I was mostly unemployed and maladjusted. I sent THOUSANDS of résumés out. I attended career fairs. I directly contacted people I wanted to work for via LinkedIn. A career counselor gave my résumé a facelift. I straight up went to Microsoft's Bay Area office and handed some bubbly receptionist my résumé.

Well my résumé was strong enough to get me to the first interview in a lot of places. I made it to initial phone interviews with Facebook, Pinterest and Yelp!. I would reach these interviews to have some hipstery 23-year-old ask if I could program HTML, how good was my Python, if I had at least 5 years of experience in a leadership position, and if my asshole could whistle "The Star Spangled Banner" in 12 languages. Then she threw my résumé into a pile of the 87 people she had to choose from, thanked me for my time, and offered the job to another 23-year-old hipster girl. "Because, like, I totally have that same top from American Apparel!" I'm a published author! I made Dean's List at Columbia! I was on TV in Japan! Thank you, Sparky, but we'll hire the guy who'll work for $6 a month and live on just the crushed dreams of hippies that we evicted (they had to move to Oakland or Portland).

After my first few months on the dole in San Francisco, I was trying everything I could think of. With each passing moment I was getting older and my FICO score was getting lower. I also aged myself out of candidacy for most entry level jobs—employers now saw me as overqualified in the wrong areas and inexperienced in the things they actually needed. Someone who needed to be paid too much for what they were asking me to do.

# Mary Ann Singleton Can Suck It

Enjoying your life in San Francisco boils down to, I believe, a question of logistics. A longtime San Francisco resident and friend put it to me this way: "Sure if you can live and work and party in the city, life is grand. Not that it often works out that way." At one point in the not too distant past, this was altogether plausible—like in the '70s. For example sake, let's look at Mary Ann Singleton from *Tales of the City*.

At the outset of *Tales*, the character Mary Ann Singleton packs her suitcase and moves to San Francisco from Ohio. This was back when the platform shoes were tall and the disco balls were glistening. In less than a week she goes from unemployed secretary to living with gaggle of super cool gay friends and smoking blunts with her groovy landlady Mrs. Madrigal. What a wonderful, fantastic, beautiful world to reinvent yourself! Some unemployed broad up and moves from Ohio and suddenly has a fabulous and exciting life in Russian Hill? Think again, sister. That San Francisco is dead.

Today Mary Ann would first have to move to Dublin-Pleasanton, a 40 minute BART ride outside the City, into a Craigslist room share owned by an "app developer" who actually deals meth in Vacaville. After searching for a decent gig for eight months, she'd land a shitty part-time temp job in San

Mateo, but she'd have to keep her side hustle working the swing shift at Ruby Tuesday to pay for the Klonopin the doctors prescribed for all the anxiety her commute is causing. She'd make some gay friends, but they'd tell her to buzz off on Saturday night. "They don't let chicks come in this bar on underwear night."

In eight months her savings would be gone, dating prospects nil, and she'd run shrieking back to Ohio.

OK maybe the picture isn't so bleak, but with the world moving to San Francisco these days, I advise people it's not nearly as easy-going and freewheeling as it was in Mary Ann's day. People who wish to move here without local contacts might consider planting a few seeds in the Bay Area first. I moved out here without any connections or a plan just like Mary Ann, and I failed spectacularly at acclimating to San Francisco at first. It's the logistics that can make or break a person here.

Also, this is not the slacker metropolis where you could "Turn on, tune in, drop out," like in the hippies' time. The Summer of Love is over. People wish to live here now because of the weather, economic prosperity, and liberal ethos, so you'll meet a lot of workers extremely overqualified for their positions and engaging in multiple side-hustles to make ends meet. That barista at Peet's Coffee? MBA from Harvard. That girl you hired on Task Rabbit to clean your house? Has a PhD from the Sorbonne in Paris. Remember that I had a BA from Columbia

I drew the line at working in fast food, but still I didn't get called back from applications to Safeway, Target, or Radio Shack. "We went with someone who is a better for the brand," was their polite way of saying, "Keep smoking crack motherfucker, we're not hiring someone with a master's degree who will simply ditch this cashier job at the first opportunity."

Always a hustler, I didn't let this stop me. I printed out a stack of résumés and pounded the pavement. Then one of those annoying-ass political canvassers approached me as I literally had four dollars to my name.

"Do you have some money to contribute to Zimbabwe Cockatoos with Malaria Foundation?"

"Look, hunty, I don't have money to buy a pack of Trident let alone cash to save your goddamn cockatoos. So you can take your crunchy, dated, granola-tie-dye and stupid fucking clipboard and shove it right up your hairy—"

"You don't have a job? We're totally hiring!"

Today companies such as Fund for the Public Interest and Grassroots Campaigns get tapped to do street canvassing to raise funds on behalf of groups such as the ACLU and Planned Parenthood. Greenpeace is actually unique because they handle their own canvassing in-house rather than outsourcing their canvassing efforts. These groups will give a job to almost anyone willing to stand on the street with a clipboard and beg for money. It's not an easy job to keep, though, because understandably the burnout rate is high.

On a positive note, street canvassing is important because it is a great way to educate the unfamiliar and put a human face on an organization. You don't think of it merely as the ACLU or Greenpeace anymore—a faceless lobbying group that you hear about in the news. It is the ACLU to whom you happily give money as they employ groovy neo-hippies like Martika who you met over at Haight and Octavia.

On a negative note, people usually think street canvassers are annoying as fuck, especially if you are in a hurry. Local San Francisco people avoid street canvassers like the Bubonic Plague, and let's be honest. Canvassers can be the political version of those people selling Dead Sea Bath Salts at any American shopping mall, trying to seduce you with an overly eager grin. Much like the beautiful Sirens in Homer's *The Odyssey*, these bitches just wanna lure you over there so they can eat you for dinner.

Should you be ensnared by one of the canvassers be warned—they are organized and have practiced their scripted "rap" on each other for several hours before meeting you that day. They have canned responses for every possible thing you can say, and the experienced canvassers are masters of these techniques. I suspect these canned responses have been crafted by marketing experts with PhD's in Freudian analysis, since the rap has the goal of manipulating your emotions and bilking

YOU for as much cash as possible. Knowing the general public is completely unaware of this emotional bear trap created by the canvassing companies, I held onto the rap for the canvassing I did for the Frida Kahlo Association for Dolphins of the Yucatan just so you can see what I'm talking about. First you lay out the trap by building your case and showing why there is a pressing need:

Opening Rap:

"My name is Charles St. Anthony, and I'm working on behalf of the Frida Kahlo Association for Dolphins of the Yucatan. I'm here today because the dolphins are dying. The Japanese are eating them as sushi and dolphin tempura. Also, Burrito Con Flipper is gaining popularity in taquerias across Mexico. Did you know that every time a bell rings, a dolphin gets its wings? A dead dolphin that is."

These are responses people would generally say to canvassers:

"Great! I'll look it up online."

To which the canvasser must respond:

"You can always check it out online, but it makes a much bigger difference when you make a contribution to a canvasser. I was able to meet you and educate you about this great cause, because of donations of people like you. We're here for the dolphins. The ones that are dying, because you don't love them enough. In Mexico."

Another common response we would get was:

"I'm already a member."

To which the canvasser must respond:

"Great! That's so awesome. We are out today to get people involved at every level of the organization. Why don't you just give me your credit card now and let me call you my bitch, because I'm not letting you go until I take you to the cleaners. I'll sign you up to contribute $90 per month! Just hand me your Amex right now you stingy sonofabitch, because if you don't Taco Bell will start offering Dolphin Chalupas next month. So stop being an asshole and fork over your card. What would Frida Kahlo say if she saw you were such a cheap ass motherfucker? *'¡Que pendejo!'* is what Frida would say, God rest her soul."

OK, I embellished that last one just a tad, but you get the gist. This is what I was reduced to after appearing for years on Japanese TV and spending $100,000 on higher education so I could live a better life. Sure the organizations were wonderful and my karma was off the hook. But I often just felt like a glorified street beggar.

My first day, I staked out a section of 3rd Street near Yerba Buena Gardens. I reminisced about how just recently I had been partying with Asian celebrities and translating interviews with stars like Olivia Newton-John and the Pussycat Dolls. Even if the cause was a good one, I couldn't shake the feeling I had taken a substantial fall from grace. *How many dolphins can I save with a $20 one time contribution anyway? These dolphins are seriously fucked. How could things get any worse?* Then I thought about having to move into my parents' basement in the Kansas City suburbs if I didn't make money. OK, that's worse. This thought truly rattled me. "Can't hack it in the Big City, huh? I guess you weren't cut out for it," my cousin Mandy would berate me. "Let's go for a snow cone." It was sink or swim time, and it turns out I could...doggie paddle.

I got complete strangers to dole out $71 that first day. Not quite the daily quota of $140 you needed to keep your job, but still a decent showing my trainers praised me. I became the Dolphins of the Yucatan Messiah for the next three weeks, bringing in hundreds of dollars a day. I am going to SAVE EVERY DOLPHIN! The generous people of San Francisco donated boatloads to save these bloody dolphins. One night Poseidon himself emerged from the depths of the ocean floor to say, "Charles, you are pretty bad ass! The dolphins of the world love you." So my luck continued this way for about a month, and then it ran out. I had a day in which I had zero dollars in contributions.

"Two more days like this, and you will get fired," the management warned me. "You have to make quota."

The next day I only made $7. To keep my job the final day of my probation I would have had to pull in $450 to make up for this. "The dolphins are counting on you," the manager guilt-tripped me. "Soon the dolphins will be extinct because your lazy ass couldn't raise enough money."

I made $6 that last day, and they cut me a check for the day's work and fired me. "Dolphin killer!" the manager said as I slinked out the door.

I felt good about it though. I was learning what the universe wanted me to discover in San Francisco: I found I could succeed at things I never imagined I was capable of. Or at least half ass them sufficiently!

# Silicon Valley of the Dolls

A year into my life in San Francisco, I got my first substantial job. This was after being fired for losing my cool with the Mongolian She-Beast and by the canvassing company for not making my daily begging quota. I got called to Oakland by a headhunter specializing in Japanese/English bilinguals. The job was to be an airline corporate sales rep at a company we'll call Asiatica Airlines. They needed someone bilingual and dependable, and I found my colleagues at Asiatica an amicable bunch. It's just the daily grind was not one I enjoyed. I lived for working with creative people in media, and I'll readily agree that this job was not a fit for me. I just worried, though, as this was my third job since returning to America, and I started to feel like I would never find my tribe.

Out of financial necessity, I started my job as a corporate airline sales rep. Yes, the job was as boring as it sounds. I arrived for the interview in Oakland and the office building had a duck pond. There were little green Cheetos all over the ground, and I realized right away that those were no Cheetos. They were duck turds that had turned green from the ducks eating grass. I just knew this was a bad omen as I walked up to this charmless office building covered in green duck shit.

After the interview, I thought *this job totally blows but I totally nailed that interview*. I got a job offer the next week, and though Asiatica was based in Oakland, I would have to drive around my sales territory, which was mostly in Silicon Valley.

Some people would have absolutely loved this job. It involved offering airline discounts to large corporations—basically if you are a major corporation that spends millions on air travel every year, then airlines offer discounts to the companies if they spend a certain percent of their air travel with them. If you were an airplane geek that jizzes yourself talking about seat "pitch" (that's the angle your seat reclines) on a Boeing 777 and which route is the fastest route from San Jose to Hyderabad, you would LOVE this job. And airplane geeks like this do exist as I found out, so I heartily recommend they apply to work at Asiatica.

The dating, the book writing, and the job searching were all happening simultaneously so there is substantial overlap with all the sections of this book—hence I was finishing the paperback of *Impossibly Glamorous* while working full time at this Asian airline. I gained thirty pounds during this era, because I was unhappy and I am an emotional eater. I would spend a full day at the airline, commute in my car from two to four hours every day, then I would sit at home in front of a computer editing and reworking my book. I would drive to Taco Bell after work for days on end and just binge eat chalupas (carefully checking that they didn't contain Mexican dolphin meat). After eating 5,000 empty calories I made sure to wash it all down with a large Diet Pepsi—a girl has to watch her figure after all. If this were the high school cafeteria in the movie *Mean Girls*, I would not sit at the table with art freaks like Janice Ian nor would I sit with the Plastics. I would have a seat at the table for "Girls Who Eat Their Feelings."

The guy with the face tattoo working at the Taco Bell in Burlingame kept asking if I was a Mormon missionary because of the cheap looking suits I'd roll up in. My money was being spent on gas, and rent, and lit lawyers. It was a very difficult era—like *Les Miserables* difficult. I was like the Fantine of flying the friendly skies. I would drive up in a rusty Corolla which dripped oil, while all the Big New Money in Silicon Valley zoomed past me in their Teslas and Corvettes.

We're mostly going to skip this year of my life, because messing with a major airline like Asiatica would make their Dementor-like lawyers descend upon me and assfuck me so hard in court I'd disappear into another dimension. So I'll just say that while I personally didn't find this job fulfilling, what a wonderful, spectacular, and fabulous company Asiatica Airlines is! Boy, oh boy! Next time I fly to Bangalore, India, I'm definitely flying Asiatica. The Asian Chicken Salad with Crispy Wonton Crunchies they serve in Premium Economy is *DIVINE!* Lawyers, if you are reading this, Asiatica is super-duper swell, and aside from the green duck turds outside the office, going to work was almost like going to Disneyland every day.

My sales territory was primarily Silicon Valley, so I would tool around every day making sales calls to admins and travel managers in the area. If you work at Facebook in Menlo Park or Apple at 1 Infinite Way in Cupertino, life is stellar. The buildings are beautiful, the workers look happy, and they truly live up to their reputation as the citadels of 21st century technological magnificence. Stanford, residing in stately Palo Alto, also exudes a sort of excellence that I personally find intoxicating. The rest of Silicon Valley is kind of a dump though. Most other office buildings in Silicon Valley have uglier décor than a Comfort Inn in Sioux City, Iowa. And even at Comfort Inn you get free cable and morning flapjacks for only $5.99. In Silicon Valley, $5.99 will buy you a single, solitary lonely-ass blueberry flapjack that will laugh in your face and diss you for not having a PhD from Stanford, MIT or one of the Ivies.

It was drab, boring, chintzy, and nothing like that fraudulent version of Silicon Valley depicted in that Facebook movie *The Social Network*. David Fincher's movie about the creation of Facebook makes placid and calm Palo Alto look like some hypersexual titty extravaganza across from the Sands Casino in Vegas. So, yeah, Silicon Valley is generally pretty boring outside those amazing companies, but the throbbing pulse of the startup and tech economy definitely reverberates through the region. That's why I find it entirely understandable that the San Francisco 49ers—a sports team named after the men who rushed out to SF in 1849 to dig for gold—moved their stadium to the heart of Silicon Valley. The 49ers now kick off in Santa Clara, where the Gold Rush of the 21$^{st}$ Century is taking place. The fortunate are cashing in on this digital boom and pricing out the residents. Many others were like me though—working long hours at a full-time job and still barely able to make rent.

Being a graduate of Columbia, I did find it incredibly frustrating that many of my fellow alumni were making mint in Silicon Valley while I was struggling to convince the VP at Rinky Dink Semiconductors that he really did want to fly Premium Economy on his next trip to Pyongyang. "Ermahgerd, the seat pitch in Asiatica's Premium Economy is about half an inch more, and you don't want the same seat pitch as the plebes flying in coach to Pyongyang, do you? Didn't think so." (I say this as a person who has only flown coach the entirety of my life). After I had put in a good 12 months, I felt it was safe to leave without creating a major hole in my résumé. I chucked deuces at Asiatica and looked for work in San Francisco again.

# You Say Portola, I Say Crapola

Much like Rosebud in Citizen Kane, someday in the future when I dance off into the great gay bar in the sky, people will have to pry a small silver metal badge from my cold dead hands. A badge which reads Passenger Vehicle Driver 72762. I'm really proud of that fucking thing. Let me explain.

This sharp-edged metal trinket was not only a badge of honor, but also symbolized my returning mojo. After ditching the airline, I did a seasonal translation job at a financial firm in downtown San Francisco where they plopped a stack of Japanese reports on a desk then told me and the other Japanese/English bilinguals to sort through it and write reports. We worked furiously for a month, but then the season for that type of report ended so we all got laid off. And you know what laid off means? FUNEMPLOYMENT BENEFITS!

This unemployment period was kind of magical, as I felt I had been rushing for the last 35 years in life. Always rushing to accomplish something. In Japanese, the character for "busy" (*isogashii*) is made of parts which mean "to lose (something)" and "heart." Literally, you are saying a busy person loses their heart, which can be true of people whose busy behavior becomes embodied in their heartlessness. For me, I felt like I had been on a hamster wheel since Pre-K and never had a moment to just chill. School, college, grad school, work, write, date, fuck, buy, sell, jump, hustle, go, go, go, go, go.

I was tired of "doing"—I just wanted to "exist" for a while.

To keep your unemployment benefits in California, you have to fill out a form every couple weeks reporting on your job hunt. I kind of wanted to relax for a minute, so I applied for a few things I might not have been qualified for. So what if I was a little inexperienced to apply to be the CEO of JP Morgan? I was still going to send my résumé in—printed on pink stationery with frog stickers. That they wouldn't hire me was entirely the HR goon's fault. Couldn't JP Morgan hire me as CEO for my inner beauty?

My schedule during unemployment consisted of a lot of drinking beer and eating pizza, and when I was bored I could walk to the café at Whole Foods.

"Score!" said the barista at Whole Foods with pink hair and a septum piercing.

She gave me the thumbs up when she saw the undecorated Bank of America debit card the unemployment office sends you. I used it to pay for my wheat grass smoothie.

"I had that card last year. It was awesome."

# Suicide Is Not the Answer

I did have major bouts of depression during this unemployed year. It was fun in some ways, but quite frustrating in others. Then I had an epiphany regarding suicide that prompted me to start this writing project. I considered deleting this chapter, as some might find it disturbing, but I know suicide is a problem in the LGBTQ community—especially among teens—so I thought it was important to leave it in here, as the message of perseverance might reach someone who needs to read it.

I think most people with some depth to their personality have thought about suicide.

I have never attempted it, but I certainly have suffered depression as I watched everyone around me slalom through life with relative ease while I spent a lot of time feeling maladjusted and out of sync with those around me. I don't intend to commit suicide as I am far too educated on the matter—people who attempt suicide usually don't die. For example, those that try to kill themselves with sleeping pills usually just sleep a lot. In most cases they survive and possibly suffer brain damage. Hanging oneself might work, but you might end up living with a broken neck. Gunshots to the head, jumping off of buildings and virtually every way to attempt suicide has ways for the attempt to backfire with only 1 in 25 suicide attempts proving successful. Cleopatra must have chosen the right asp, as she could have woken up a few days later with a bad headache, a swollen titty, and a shitload of Roman legions at the doorstep of Egypt. Suicide as they say is a "permanent solution to a temporary problem," and if you fail at attempting suicide, you run the risk of simply multiplying your problems like the Mogwai in *Gremlins* after a dip in the pool.

It wasn't any one person or any one defeat, but there were many times in San Francisco I felt I didn't want to take another step forward. I didn't want another résumé rejected. More than putting a gun to my head, I wanted to crawl under my desk, pull a cloak of oblivion over my head, and disappear.

Now Charles, you may be thinking, what's with all this navel gazing horse shit? Where's the "King of Queens" who appeared on Japanese TV? Where's the *joie de vivre*? We didn't buy your sassy gay book for all this Sylvia Plath meets Emily the Strange drivel! We don't need this existential crap. You're not fucking Foucault!

OK, Dear Reader, we'll get back to the sass in a second, but occasionally I have the prerogative to write a sass-free chapter!

The world keeps telling you you're not smart enough for the job. Not attractive enough to find an honest mate. Not cool enough to be in the clique. Not not not not not. Sometimes, when the Army of Nots shows up at your doorstep, it's hard to shoo them away. And it is frustrating because people will tell you to "think positive" all the time and use the *Law of Attraction* or other such New Age philosophy. Those things can be helpful in terms of focusing on what you want out of life, but sometimes it's a lot like telling a heroin junkie to "Just Say No." A serious psychological problem needs to be addressed with more than an emotional Band-Aid, and what's going on can't be fixed just by making a Vision Board. I got through my depression by reading about cognitive therapy and a couple months on Zoloft. Some cardio helped as well getting my natural endorphins flowing.

The following realization finally ended my walk through the emotional darkness. One of these days that I was unemployed and busy with activities such as watching clips of Wendy Williams on YouTube, I stumbled onto a site relating to one person's escape from suicidal thoughts. He or she thought about how this manner of thought was offensive to evolution. If you think about it, billions of years of coincidence and evolution have gone into creating you. So moping about and thinking of suicide is offensive to the trilobites from 500 million years ago. Offensive to the first legged fish that gasped for oxygen on land and became amphibians. Offensive to the dinosaurs that put the ASS in Jurassic (copyright Charles). Offensive to the first mammals, the first monkeys, the woolly mammoths, and the saber tooth tigers. The Neanderthals, the *Homo erectus,* and the first man. It was offensive to all these creatures which had toiled, labored, and fought to become me. Five billion years of evolution went into creating me, and now you're just going to lay there because the chips are down and the money is flowing the wrong way? Get. The. Fuck. Up.

I will add I began to feel it was also offensive to my ancestors. The ones that braved small pox, and a weeks-long voyage over the Atlantic in a boat to start a new life in the USA. Certainly they faced pestilence, hunger, unsanitary conditions, and all that shit on the Oregon Trail which always sounded so terrifying. Then you have the veterans in my family who fought during WWII so that guys like myself—an unseen descendent they would never meet—could thrive. Alright, my grandparents faced fucking Hitler. I can deal with a few rejections and bruised ego. Time to stand back up, hold my head tall, and stride forth courageously into the world.

# Bringing Back the Mojo

After a good five months taking this funemployment time out, I realized that while it was enjoyable being lazy, I wasn't getting laid. In San Francisco, no money means no honey, and I was getting too old to spin my flaxen locks into gold by landing a Sugar Daddy. I was a Daddy now—a DILF if you will—the only Sugar Daddy on the block was going to be me. And to be that, I definitely needed a job.

I was over trying to find someone to "hire" me though. My first book, *Impossibly Glamorous,* was now for sale, and I knew that having a book in which I drop F bombs on the first page and talks about anal waxing was probably not the thing most HR managers looked for. In fact, I'm certain my book sent several human resources specialists shrieking off into the night.

Beyond the employment issues I had before, I realized I should try my luck creating my own Yellow Brick Road ahead. Build my own platform. Reach for the stars.

I didn't know quite where to turn, so I went to a local chapter of Debtors Anonymous at a nearby church, as I figured they would discuss places to procure employment. A friend I made there suggested I drive a taxi, because, "Cab drivers can totally make $30 per hour."

At first I winced at the idea, because I'd rather drive a tugboat off Niagara Falls than drive a taxi. Not that this was my only possible path ahead. Armani Exchange had offered to make me seasonal worker as it was near Christmas. But did I want to fold T-shirts with a bunch of snippy queens for minimum wage, or did I want to make $30 per hour cruising the City in my sweet yellow ride?

Then it struck me: driving a taxi in San Francisco would be a comedy goldmine and provide great material for my follow up to *Impossibly Glamorous*. The die had been cast—I would drive a taxi. That's how much I love you, Dear Reader. I love you enough to risk life and limb driving a dirty-ass San Francisco taxi cab.

Getting the job as a taxi driver was a lot harder than I realized. You must take a set of courses at a "Certified Taxi School" so you have a minimum knowledge of city streets and landmarks (this takes a week or two). There are the FBI fingerprint checks which I imagine are pretty lax because there are some sketchy-ass taxi drivers in San Francisco.

Then you have to go to get an "intent to hire" letter from a taxi company, go to a lecture from the bicycle association, and finally take another exam at the SFMTA. Including the Certified Taxi School, the exam fee, transport to class, Livescan background check and other fees, I spent around $500 to become a yellow cab driver, and it took around a month. You can start to understand why taxi drivers detest rideshare drivers who slap a pink mustache on their cars and call themselves "drivers." I know the process at Lyft, Uber and Sidecar is more involved than that, but considering getting a taxi permit was more complicated than applying to Dartmouth or Stanford, I'm surprised there isn't flat out violence in the streets with taxi drivers burning the Lyft logo in effigy.

There was one taxi driver I met from Nigeria who would take the Lyft logos off of cars and cast some Nigerian voodoo onto them. He would steal a Lyft mustache, douse it in goat's blood, and chant, "Mustache of Satan, Drivers of Baphomet! Begone! Begone!" I'm not sure what effect this had, but it makes a pretty good cocktail party conversation piece.

Personally, in San Francisco I prefer the non-profit Homobile—a rideshare service for LGBTQ riders that touts itself as "Moes gettin' hoes where they needz to goes." To translate that for straight people, that means, "We are homos who take people places they want to go." They have a suggested donation rate you pay at the end, and whether you are in full blown drag, dressed up in fetish gear, or just can't get a taxi to take you and your trick home from the Castro, the Homobile is there to drive you home and infinitely less judgey than the possibly horrifying taxi ride that may be waiting for you.

The taxi school enlightened me, though. We had to memorize the order of the streets in certain areas which we did with a series of mnemonic devices. My personal favorite was for the Tenderloin, which is "Very Pretty Ladies Have Lost

Jewelry" which stands for "Van Ness, Polk, Larkin, Hyde, Leavenworth, Jones." These streets cover an area where the Very Pretty Ladies might actually be girls with something *extra special*. In addition to the jewelry the Very Pretty Ladies might have lost, some of them have lost their pride, dignity, dreams, hygiene, sanity, underwear, testicles, and crack pipes. Driving across these streets via Post Street near Divas nightclub late at night was possibly my favorite part of being a taxi driver, as the Trans street walkers along this stretch are always turnt, even if they might have lost their jewelry.

There were some interesting laws that apply to taxi drivers and passengers in San Francisco that I was completely unaware of. For example, of course the drivers aren't supposed to drink booze, but taxi passengers in SF legally can have open containers of alcohol with them as they ride.

The laws pertaining to animals also intrigued me. San Francisco provides a system called Paratransit where people with disabilities receive a debit card good for a certain amount of money to use in taxis. When a passenger with a disability is boarding the taxicab, drivers are not allowed to ask what disability they have. If someone is trying to board with their service animal, you are legally able to ask, "What service does this animal provide?" There are a lot of asshole dog owners in San Francisco who will lie and try to say their mutt is a service animal. I would ask them what service the animal provided, and if they be like, "This is my Spirit Animal," I'd politely tell them to get the fuck out of my taxi cab.

Telling them to buzz off wasn't totally legal. The law regarding animals riding in cabs in San Francisco states that as long as the animal is orderly and not bouncing around, taxis must provide transportation. I'm just glad the crazy people in San Francisco don't generally know these laws, because I was just waiting for someone to try to transport their black mamba or warthog in my cab and act like everything is kosher.

Like I mentioned before, I spent around $500 and it took about a month to get my A Card (taxi permit), which may seem like a long time, but that's child's play compared to some cities. In London, taxi drivers must run a gauntlet that includes passing a test called "The Knowledge." Wikipedia suggests that it takes 34 months or an average of 12 attempts to pass The Knowledge.

Basically all you need to know to be a San Francisco taxi driver is to always turn left onto Franklin Street. There is nowhere to turn left on Market Street for about two miles between Franklin Street and Front Street. It depends on where you start your journey, but many fares going to Union Square, North Beach or Russian Hill have to go up Franklin (which has a long stretch of well-timed green lights), then cut across the city. Tourists sometimes got scared when I went up Franklin to shimmy over as they didn't realize that San Francisco has this Fatwa on left turns along Market Street downtown. Of course the tourists will start bitching because they immediately suspect the cab driver is scamming them—when really hotels such as the Hilton O'Farrell, St. Regis, and the Parc 55 are often best reached by taking this Franklin route.

If I could find the man responsible for the ludicrous chaos of the SF Street layout and scald his face with a hot poker I would. The one-way streets, the sharp hills, and general confusion of the city's counterintuitive sprawl can make even the most level-headed driver foam at the mouth in automotive fury. In fact, it wasn't just one man who planned things. The conventional wisdom is there were two factions that fought over whether to make the streets of San Francisco a grid layout like most of Manhattan, or whether to make the roads fit the beautiful landscape of the City. In the end, they did half of both and it can lead the city to seem like it has split personalities. The street names often change depending on which neighborhood you are in, and even a lot of long-time residents are unaware that Turk becomes Balboa, Geneva becomes Ocean Avenue, and Castro Street unceremoniously hijacks the pathway of Divisidero. Market becomes Portola which in turn morphs into Junipero Serra. Just to put all this confusion in perspective, when arriving in Manhattan as a student, it took me about three days to learn how to access most of the island. San Francisco took me about three years.

Eventually I could zip across the city with little to no problem anytime, though while I was still new, a man once yelled at me, "Study a fucking map!" when I took some wrong turns to his Union Square Hotel. The frustrating part is once you have made a mistake, many streets downtown are one way and will force you to turn when you don't want to. My biggest downfall was always on Fourth Street near the CalTrain station, because literally every lane in this four lane clusterfuck forces you to drive somewhere different. Sure, that doesn't sound bad, but generally I found if you accidentally took the passenger across the Bay Bridge over to Oakland, you didn't get tipped very well.

# Destiny's Charles

Upon passing the taxi exam in December 2013, I started driving a couple days into 2014. "I'm not gonna have a rookie driver out on the roads on New Years' Eve. That's suicide," the manager of Golden Gate Cab snarked. Golden Gate snapped me up as soon as I completed the exam because Uber and Lyft had made the taxi companies desperate for taxi drivers. A group of taxi company owners waited outside the examination rooms, all vying to get workers from the new group of drivers. The manager at Golden Gate also was gay, so I felt comfortable going to work for them. They weren't going to question me if I mostly waited for fares from my LGBTQ brethren in the Castro.

Not that taxi companies employ that strict of a management system. You show up, you pay the rental fee (called the "Gate"), you check your car and you go. I got the luxury of tooling around town in a new Ford Escape hybrid, which I handled much more easily than the Toyota Prius. Most of the other drivers were honest immigrants simply providing for the families. Some guys drove taxis, because it allowed them to have a lifestyle with total freedom in their personal lives. Other drivers, and there is no delicate way to put this, were straight up mutants or fringe people. The taxi lot itself was disgusting. Tons of pigeon shit that came from a highway overpass up above created a line straight through the parking lot. The gates for each company vary, but I generally found them to be $80 - $125 per shift; Sunday mornings were cheap while Saturday nights were the most expensive. When you added the fees you paid for cleaning and filling up the tank with gas, most days started with you in the hole and it could be four or five hours before I ever made any profit. Of course, the first part of your profit needed to be held onto to pay the next day's gate.

My first day out, the manager recommended I hit North Beach and Embarcadero since tourists wouldn't be in as much of a hurry as jaded city folk. I drove straight to the Castro instead. My first fare was a jovial Australian couple going to the Fairmont Hotel—a hotel that Michelle Obama is rumored to stay in. The first ride was entirely unremarkable except for the fact that I was so excited to get my first fare, I got caught up in chatting with the couple and forgot to turn on the taxi meter.

Realizing my mistake, I bargained at the end of the ride. "Does twelve dollars sound fair to you?"

"Here's a twenty! Drive safe now and make lots of money." God bless Australia! The most quiche country on the planet.

The fact that the first fare were from abroad brings up something important. Due to the fact that yellow cabs are now passé, most fabulous young San Franciscans now stick to Uber and Lyft. The people still riding in taxi cabs could fit into one of several categories. First you have people from places where ride sharing has not caught on yet, such as foreigners or American yokels that are from places without cabs. Then you have people with bad credit. Just like they say "No money, no honey," you could say "No credit card, no Uber." This means a lot of prostitutes rode in my taxi cab, because they depend on a cash economy. I am very respectful of sex industry workers and think it should be legal. Hookers could be a lot of fun, but they are not generally known for being fiscally responsible—which is why some of them didn't have credit cards or smart phones to use Uber.

Other types of people who still use cabs are the people who need a ride RIGHT THIS VERY SECOND. For example, people who fight with their boyfriends and leave a club or a restaurant upset. Then you have people whose cell phones have run out of batteries.

Bringing the discussion back to foreigners, quite a few British citizens rode in my taxi cab. For the most part, they were delightful and charming, but there were a few of the moaners who always had something negative to say. That's fine by me. I understand that moaning is a sort of a bonding experience they enjoy in the UK akin to cricket. I personally love a good rant, as long as there's a dash of wit and a sprinkle of humor to make it entertaining—so basically I had a good time with my British riders.

The British visitors' biggest complaint was that they found US service to be suffocating. They understood Americans work for tips, but they really did not want the server to check on them after every nibble of pizza or sip of Perrier.

"How do you Americans even get a bite to eat?" one woman from Canterbury asked me. "I have nothing to ask for. I just ordered my chimichanga, I don't need a second cocktail right this second." Having been to London a couple times myself, I understood that British service people gave customers more breathing space, and that a higher base salary eliminates the need for tips. In fact, service in Britain can be shockingly rude at times, so I decided to bully my British passengers and be mean to them as a marketing strategy to get better tips. And it worked.

"We've arrived. Out of my car you Pommie bastard!" I said to a couple from Brighton as they got out at Fisherman's Wharf.

"Now that's a fine chap. Here you go." The man tipped me with a twenty pound note. That's like a thirty dollar tip, mind you. Score!

"This cab has a no wankers allowed policy. You need to get out NOW!" I berated a man from Coventry.

"You're hilarious. Next drink when you get off is on me," and he handed me a fifty.

Giving bad service to British people turned out to be really lucrative. I kept it up.

This strategy did not always work. "Where are you chav-tastic cunts going?" Chav is British slang for "white trash."

"I believe we'll be getting out here," said a blonde with knee-high leather boots.

"Sod off then, Emma Bunton. Slappers like you are a pestilence!"

"Some mouth you've got. I've a mind to report you to your manager."

So despite the fact that British complain that American service is suffocating, I learned that at times, British people do in fact want nice service.

In addition to the Brits and Aussies, I had a smattering of French, Mexicans, Brazilians, Spaniards, Filipinos and more. I wasn't just a taxi driver, I was the Goddamn United Nations.

The only group that basically lived up to their stereotype every single time they got in my taxi were the Irish. Not Irish Americans mind you, Irish from actual Ireland. They were consistently hammered in a bad way, and they would get unruly and obnoxious or pass out in the cab and not be able to say where they were going. I've had my days where I have gotten way too plastered myself, so I can't really get on any soapbox. But seriously, the nation of Ireland needs to start going to AA. If they can convert the entire city of Cork into a rehab center like Promises or Betty Ford, I think things will start to improve. I feel safe saying this, because like most US citizens I am a delightful genetic mutt with like 1/32 of my ancestry coming from the Emerald Isle. Just like my Irish cousins I am sort of an expert on being too drunk in a taxi (as a passenger not a driver of course).

One time this Irish bloke got in my taxi and I recalled him from a previous time he had gotten way too drunk and ridden with me. I remembered where he lived in the Outer Sunset, so I started on my way. We chatted nicely at first, but he eventually stopped talking. After about ten minutes of silence, I looked in the rearview mirror to see his mouth hanging wide open and a blank stare on his face. Drool had started cascading down the side of his chin. *Oh crap, if this Irish fucker dies in my taxi cab, I won't make very good tips tonight.*

When we stopped outside his condo, he snapped awake and paid me like nothing had happened. He got out of the car. Then I heard an enormous thud as the 6-foot-something Irish gentleman came crashing down like the Jolly Green Giant in a spell of narcolepsy.

I got out, helped him stumble over to his door, then drove off.

# The Butterflies of the Night

I loved driving at night. After nine or so, a type of pixie dust sprinkled down across the city. Everyone I picked up after this hour I could assume had a couple drinks in them, and generally were out to enjoy themselves. One thing I also noticed is that crack heads really like motorized wheelchairs, and I would see people flying across Market Street downtown at very odd hours. When I saw guys popping wheelies in their motorized wheelchairs at 3 a.m., I would think to myself, *Shuffles must have gotten ahold of some good crack tonight.*

Usually I spent a lot of my night in the Castro. And I could generally count on a group of drunk gay men going home from a night of partying to make jokes about vaginas within three minutes of getting in the cab.

"Oh, driver, my pussy is on fire. You need to turn on that air conditioner."

"Girl, if you're coochie is burning up, maybe you best take that business to the doctor. Ain't no air conditioner in the world that can help you if your cooze is radioactive!"

I don't know what it is about gay men and vagina jokes, but it was always entertaining nonetheless.

Working the Castro was great for my self-esteem, as I got hit on almost every night. I played hard to get until the guys were literally grabbing me. I knew that there were some major liability factors involved. I totally made out with cute guys in the back of my taxi once they asked me to, but I stopped short of penetration. Taxis are all fitted with security cameras nowadays, and I didn't want Amir back at Golden Gate Taxi to have a heart attack if he checked the camera footage. But I left the meter running—that was one ride those bitches were gonna pay for.

The running joke amongst drag queens who rode with me is that GPS would be much cooler if they had a drag queen's voice. How cool would Siri be if that bitch could read you like Shangela in *RuPaul's Drag Race*? "Oh, girl you can't turn left here. Can't turn left at the next street neither. Bitch, don't you know this is San Francisco, better get yo' ass over to Arco and get you some premium unleaded before we all get stranded in the Tenderloin. Halleloo!"

Friday nights were generally the most fun, as I could crank up the jams and facilitate people's nighttime adventures to the best of my ability. The nonstop eighties mix Friday night on 98.1 Kiss FM got the best reviews, as people might complain about having house or hip hop music on, but everyone loves the eighties—at least for a twelve minute cab ride on a Friday night.

A person could be the biggest prick in the universe, but will start dancing like a complete dumbass the minute "Walk Like an Egyptian" by the Bangles starts playing. "Don't You Want Me" by Human League always started a cab ride sing-along and helped me get bigger tips. Anyway, I guess the thing I liked about cab driving is I got to be part of nightlife without getting fucked up myself. I was the designated driver for a city of 830,000 people, and it was a blast.

Drunk straight women tended to either be incredibly fun or incredibly annoying. Generally the cuter the girl, the bigger the problem she could be as these women were used to parlaying their feminine charms to get things for free. About once a week, I would get a bitch who would pretend to forget she had gotten in a taxi and try to get out without paying.

"I'm so used to Uber, I forgot I was in a taxi cab."

"Hunty, you saw the yellow car. You stretched your scrawny arm way up in the air and waved it up and down until I stopped. Then you opened the door and got in the cab. Now I just drove your Lululemon ass thirty minutes to the Marina. Fork over the cash, you raggedy heffa!" This is not what I would say because I wanted to get tips, but I was thinking it. And I know these women were lying because drunk men never did this, while women pulled these shenanigans on the regular.

The best tippers tended to be straight men with a girl they wanted to impress. Then women and LGBT people who appreciated my fabulosity. The worst tippers were foreigners and the elderly. You can't blame people on fixed income, but the foreigners pissed me off sometimes. I know some foreigners are not used to tips, but others were obviously feigning ignorance to get off cheap.

As mentioned before, streetwalkers, escorts and other types of sex professionals were among the people who rode my taxis regularly. I quite enjoyed taking prostitutes to meet johns at hotels simply because they occupy a social space so foreign to me.

Not that the women ever came right out and declared, "I'm selling my cooter tonight." But if I got a fare that was an overly-made-up young woman with skin that suggested heavy drug use—heading to a hotel alone late at night—I understood that these ladies were doing something strange for a little change.

They differed from the non-pro girls who were just dressed seductively for a night on the town. In true *Belle de Jour* style, the escorts would usually wear a coat or something to cover up as they entered the hotels so as to *not* draw attention to themselves. It was all done with a wink and a nudge, and the girls would give me tips as to which hotels to stay in. From my extremely un-scientific poll of the pro girls of San Francisco, apparently the beds are little too hard at the Parc 55 and the Ritz Carlton was voted the whore favorite.

The most memorable ride in my taxi career was with a Tenderloin prostitute. She had crunchy bleached hair, and I knew I had made a mistake when she wanted to ride with her pushcart in my car. Her pushcart was one of the small wire types that are truly *en vogue* with elderly Asian women.

Jolene wanted a ride out to Golden Gate Park to pick up a fridge she had found on Craigslist that someone was throwing out. The Craigslist poster said she could have it for free if she just came to pick it up. So we drove toward Golden Gate Park. She was sort of twitching in the way that meth addicts do. We picked up the dorm fridge and had a nice discussion about the online ads she used to work as an escort.

She asked to go to an SRO on a particularly seedy section of Ellis Street. SRO stands for Single Residence Occupancy Hotel, but these hotels are not like the Best Western or Holiday Inn. These are places where many vagrants and junkies stay. I knew better than to wait long outside as the drug dealers and other unsavory characters hang out and watch closely as you exchange handfuls of cash for the taxi fare.

So I did what I normally did when I took someone to an SRO in the Tenderloin.

"Look Jolene! It's your lucky day. I'm giving you a discount. Just give me $20 instead of the $30 it says on the meter and we'll call it even. Just have your payment ready when we get to your place so I can drive off quickly," I said.

I turned off the meter and Jolene immediately started pitching a fit, "Why the fuck did you turn off the meter? You think my money is not good enough for you. Turn the meter back on. I oughta get you fucking fired." I was not in the mood for life lessons from a meth whore.

We arrived at the SRO, and of course a sleazy group of gangsters were hanging out by the front porch and talking about Cheez-Its. Adrenaline pumped through my body. I flew out of the cab, tossed the refrigerator at the front door, and ran back to the car.

The problem with meth addicts is they can't ever find shit. Jolene spent fifteen minutes rifling through her raggedy purse with bits of garbage, Mentos wrappers and condoms inside.

"Really, it's OK Jolene. Just get out of the car." A toothless vagrant rapped at my window and asked for change.

"No I have another dollar. I'm trying to find it." So far she had fished out two twisted and mangled five dollar bills that no doubt carried every contagion from hepatitis to the Ebola virus.

"No really Jolene, get out." She finally got out after giving me twelve dollars. I lost about an hour of driving time and was shorted twenty dollars on that fare, but I escaped with my life.

I sped off as the Chiva dealers waved goodbye.

# Time to Invest in Uber

The long-time cab drivers all lamented the downturn with the advent of the ridesharing model—some claimed they lost 30% or more of their business. A few taxi drivers were true hustlers who arrived at the hotels or airport at 4 a.m., and these types of drivers remained relatively unaffected. But many of the drivers crossed over to the dark side of the Force and became Lyft and Uber drivers.

The consumers' voice has spoken, though. Yellow cabs are the dinosaurs in a world overrun by mammals. People have generally had enough shitty taxi rides in their lives that they are more than happy to ditch the yellow cab to ride with the quirky Lyft driver or swanky Uber wheels. Talking about this with the owner of a taxi school, the professor told me, "In San Francisco now, the social distance between your average taxi driver and your resident is simply too vast." San Francisco is no longer a spunky Wild West backwater that the freaks and the hippies could find a safe haven in—SF is now a boutique City catering to a new class of techie bourgeoisie. And they ride Uber.

# The Ride Comes to an End

They taught us in taxi school to bring a "Puke Pack" with some air freshener, bleach, and Purell for when the inevitable happened. Though several people barfed outside of my cab, thankfully I completed my tenure as a taxi driver with only one person properly puking inside the taxi. I had my rubber gloves and puke pack, so I charged him an $100 cleaning fee (which I was legally entitled to do), and sent that motherfucker on his way.

While scrubbing the nacho cheese and stomach juices off the back seat, I began to feel this was not a good use of my master's degree. The taxi gig had served a great role in my life: I had gotten off my ass after being unemployed, made a few interesting acquaintances, and received my beautiful little taxi badge to become Passenger Vehicle Driver 72762. Please make sure when I die I'm buried with it.

I had given up on someone hiring me, but I figured I would study some tech classes at Academy X downtown and learn how to better manage my websites. I ditched the taxi company to become a security guard, which I planned on doing while I studied necessities such as SEO and WordPress. Driving a taxi is too dangerous, and I know it sounds funny that I felt being a security guard was safer, but truly there are many ways to die as a cab driver. I planned on living.

I wish I had known about security three years earlier when I arrived in San Francisco, as it only took one day of class to get the requirements to be a guard. I received my "guard card" in the mail a few weeks later, and it took one day to get a full-time job at a nice security company run by a group of Russians. All I have to say is if you need security workers please hire Russians, because they will take any dusty, rat-infested construction site and defend it like Nikita Khrushchev just walked into the Kremlin. Construction sites always need guards to keep vandals and homeless out, and with construction booming in every part of the City, there is a high demand for security workers. I always had work and could study what I wanted as I plotted my next move.

Then one day I was dicking around on Duolingo studying Brazilian Portuguese at one of my guard posts. I checked my email to see that a headhunter had contacted me. It wasn't for any job, but for THE job in Silicon Valley. At least the dream job for me. Here I had given up on finding a job the old fashioned way, and now a new pathway presented itself. So I chucked deuces at the security company and got ready to join the Gold Rush going on an hour south of San Francisco.

Because I've signed an ironclad NDA, you're not going to hear a fucking word about it! From this point forward, much like Jay-Z and Beyoncé I prefer to have my life shrouded in mystery. Where could it be? Possibly that fruit bearing company out in Cupertino? Or maybe the headhunter saw my LinkedIn profile and placed me at LinkedIn? How about that place in Menlo Park that starts with "Face" and ends with "Book?" Will Zuck and I be kicking it at the Playa during Burning Man next year?

That is for me to know and you to find out. I suppose you could plug my name into your favorite search engine and see what comes up. See you in Silicon Valley, bitches!

*Fin.*

# My Acknowledgements

Thank you for taking this journey with everyone's favorite San Francisco Daddy. Please take a moment to review this book on Goodreads or your favorite retailer!

This book is dedicated to my friends.

I especially want to thank three of you who really stood by me during this era: Kermy Girl, Gomenasai Brown, and Baby Spice. I couldn't have made it through this without you!

Merci beaucoup to my publishing friends Apollo GT, Sari Friedman, Sarah Melton, D. Patrick Miller and Synchronized Chaos online magazine. Big kiss to Bay Area publicity maven Cristina Deptula of Authors Large and Small.

Further thanks for the special support I received from Dante Cassius, Ashton Cruz, James St. James, Kamasami Kong, Peter Lackner, Mr. Palo Alto, Júnior Reis, Donna Sachet, Shar Silva, and Fushimi Tatsuya.

Kisses to all y'all bitches that light up my Instagram, Twitter and Snapchat (@kingcharles0921). There are way too many of you to name each one (and I love you all), but I will give special thanks to Roseann, Judy, Ryoko, and Sarah. I appreciate all your messages and retweets. Your love gets me through the day. See you online my lovelies!

# Author's Bio, Book and Websites

## Meet Charles St. Anthony

Charles acquired his BA from Columbia University in East Asian Studies with an emphasis on Japanese, and his MA in the same subject from Sophia University in Tokyo, Japan. He subsequently worked as a translator for American celebrities visiting Japan, appeared on Japanese TV as a foreign commentator, and even appeared in a Japanese movie called *Juoku En Kasegu!* (The Billion Yen Jackpot!). Charles lives and works in the Bay Area in Northern California.

Follow on Instagram, Twitter or Snapchat: kingcharles0921.

# First Book

## Impossibly Glamorous

(Originally released under his government name Charles Ayres)

This book is an autobiographical account of Charles' travails growing up gay in Kansas then working as a Japanese media personality in Tokyo. Hilarious, heartwarming and full of celebrity dish, check for *Impossibly Glamorous* at your favorite online retailer today! If you enjoyed *San Francisco Daddy*, you are sure to love *Impossibly Glamorous*.

# Websites

Palais Charles — www.palaischarles.com

Social and media commentary

Random Ass Shoes — www.randomassshoes.com

Crowdsourced photography for charity

Translation Geisha — www.translationgeisha.com

Analyzing trends in the news and pop culture by translating Japanese social media such as Tweets and online articles into English

www.ingramcontent.com/pod-product-compliance
Lightning Source LLC
Chambersburg PA
CBHW020620300426
44113CB00007B/725